W9-BFI-164

THE STORY OF
LIFE ON EARTH

For Edward

Published in the United States in 1999 by
The Millbrook Press, Inc.
2 Old New Milford Road
Brookfield, Connecticut 06804

Created and produced by Nicholas Harris, Joanna Turner
and Claire Aston, Orpheus Books Ltd

Illustrated by Nicki Palin

Scientific consultant: Professor Michael Benton,
Department of Geology, University of Bristol

Copyright © 1999 Orpheus Books Ltd

All rights reserved. No part of this book may be reproduced or
transmitted in any form or by any means without permission in
writing from the publisher and the copyright owner, except by a
reviewer who wishes to quote brief passages in a review.

Library of Congress Cataloging-in-Publication Data

Harris, Nicholas, 1956-
  The story of life on earth / Nicholas Harris, Nicki
Palin.
    p.   cm.
  Summary: Describes the appearance and development of
life on our planet, from tiny sea creatures through
dinosaurs and the first mammals to the arrival and
dominance of humans.
  ISBN 0-7613-1269-2 (lib. bdg.)
  1. Life--Origin--Juvenile literature. 2. Life
(Biology)--Juvenile literature. [1. Life--Origin.
2. Evolution. 3. Life (Biology)] I. Palin, Nicki.
II. Title.
QH325.H36 1999
570--dc21   98-29742
                                            CIP
                                            AC

Printed in Belgium

1 3 5 4 2

THE STORY OF
LIFE ON EARTH

Written by
NICHOLAS HARRIS

Illustrated by
NICKI PALIN

M
The Millbrook Press
Brookfield, Connecticut

Millions and millions and millions . . . and millions of years ago,

nothing lived in our world.

There were no people.
No animals.
No trees.
No grass.
No fish in the sea.

The land was just rock.

The wind howled, streams gurgled, and waves crashed on
the seashore.

But no birds sang, no lions roared, no leaves rustled in
the trees.

Millions and millions and millions of years later . . .

. . . something stirred under the sea.

At first, there were tiny jellyfish drifting in the water.
Worms wriggled around in the mud.

Then, some very strange creatures appeared.
Some had lots of legs and scuttled along the seabed.

Some had spikes and crept slowly about.

One had five mushroom-shaped eyes on its head and teeth on the end of its arm.

There was one that looked almost like a fish, but it had no fins.

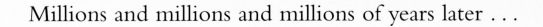

Millions and millions and millions of years later . . .

. . . the sea was
crowded with living
things.

There were creatures
that looked like
underwater beetles,
but had lots of legs.

The fish still didn't
have fins. They swam
around with their
mouths open, sucking
in things to eat.

Later, some fish did grow fins. They also had huge jaws with fearsome teeth, and went chasing after smaller creatures.

Millions and millions of years later . . .

. . . something was happening on land.

Plants had begun to grow.
At first, they stayed very close to the seashore.
Then, they spread farther and farther inland.

The land, once rocky and empty, was green at last.

Insects and creepy-crawly things fed on the plants.
Some fish that swam in the lakes and streams began to feed on *them*.

They even dashed out of the water to grab the biggest, juiciest insects.

Their fins were so strong and plump they were like legs.
Some fish could walk around on land and even breathe fresh air.

Millions and millions of years later . . .

. . . some fish found they could live on land nearly all the time.
Their fins had toes to help them walk better.
Instead of flat, fishy tails, they had long, straight ones.

These creatures went back to the water only to lay their eggs and to cool off in the heat.

Meanwhile, the plants had started to grow tall and straight.
They were the first trees.

It was hot and rainy, the sort of weather plants love.
Soon there were thick, dark forests everywhere.
Dragonflies the size of seagulls buzzed and flitted among the trees.

Wormy creatures as long as your arm and with lots of legs scuttled about.

The fish-with-legs wallowed about in the dank, dark, muddy ponds, grunting and snorting.

Meanwhile, in the high tree branches, a little animal
darted around.
Like the fish-with-legs, it had a long, smooth body.
But it looked more like a lizard.

It had learned to lay its eggs on land.
Now it didn't have to spend any time in the water at all.

It was the first reptile.

Millions and millions of years later . . .

the forest had disappeared.
It was still very hot, but now it was much drier.

Some very big reptiles lolled around, soaking up the
sunshine.
Great sails of skin rose from their backs.

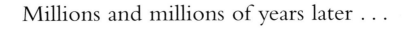

Millions and millions of years later . . .

. . . there were many different kinds of reptiles.

Some had stout, bony bodies and spiky heads.

Some had tusks and snuffled like pigs.

Some had long legs and could run very fast.

Some were quite small and grew furry coats (more about *them* later).

The long-legged reptiles found they could run even faster if they stood upright.
So they went around on their two back legs.

They had long tails to help them keep their balance. Their arms were short and strong, good for grabbing things to eat.

They were the first dinosaurs.

The dinosaurs ruled the world for millions of years.

Some kinds died out, but new ones came along to take their place.

Dinosaurs came in all shapes and sizes.
Some were just enormous.
They had very, very long necks and very, very long tails.
Altogether they were longer than three buses parked end to end.

Some dinosaurs were small, no bigger than cats.

Some, like Diplodocus, were gentle creatures, content to munch leaves all day.

Some looked very odd.
They had spikes on their backs, or horns on their heads, or clubs at the tips of their tails.

Some, like Tyrannosaurus rex, were fierce monsters. They were as tall as a house, and could run as fast as a car. They had teeth as long and sharp as daggers.

Meanwhile, those little furry creatures hid themselves away.
They dared to come out only at night while the dinosaurs were sleeping.

They were the first mammals.

Some tiny, light dinosaurs grew feathers.
They found that they could glide from tree to tree.

They were the first birds.

The birds were not alone in the skies.
Some other reptiles had gotten there first.
They had wings made of skin and large heads with long, powerful beaks.
Some of these flying reptiles grew to the size of small airplanes.

Reptiles lived in the seas as well.
Some looked like fish.
They grew fins and fishy tails to help them swim fast.
Others had long, snakelike necks.

Then every one of the dinosaurs vanished from the face of the Earth.
No one knows exactly why.

Perhaps a huge rock or block of ice from outer space crashed into our planet.

The dust and smoke from the explosion may have plunged the world into darkness for many years.

Maybe it became too cold for the dinosaurs.

At last, the mammals could come out of hiding.

Millions and millions of years later . . .

. . . there were many different kinds of mammals.

They looked almost like some animals you can see at the zoo today.

There were elephants with tusks that pointed backward instead of forward.
There were giraffes with short necks.

There were horses the size of cats.
There were guinea pigs the size of hippos.

Birds sang in the trees.
Insects hovered over flowers.

But there were still no people.

And then, millions of years later . . .

. . . the ice came.

The ice spread to many parts of the world.
Woods and meadows, plains and valleys, uplands and
lowlands, were all covered by thick ice.

Animals could live only in places that the ice didn't
reach.
It was very cold and wintry all year round.

The woolly
rhinoceros had a
thick, furry coat to
keep it warm.

The cave bear
escaped the worst of
the weather by
sleeping all through
the winter.

The mammoth was the mightiest creature in the ice kingdom.
Yet it feared another, much smaller animal.

This animal didn't have horns or sharp teeth, but it did carry spears with sharp stone blades.

Humans had arrived.

At first, people had to go looking for food in the wild, just like all the other animals.
They hunted, fished, and found nuts and berries in the forest.
They lived in caves or in tents made from branches and animal skins.

Then some people discovered how to grow plants that
they could use for food.
They also tamed some wild animals and kept them.

Now people didn't have to wander in search of things to
eat.
They could build villages and live there all the time.

Thousands of years passed.

There were more and more people.

There were more and more villages.
People cut down more and more trees to make room for their crops and their animals.

They hunted animals with guns, and trapped fish in huge nets.

Some of the villages grew into towns and then cities.

People built railways, roads, bridges, and airports.
They dug large holes in the ground.

People needed more space.

Animals that live in the wild need space, too.
But people usually get their way, so many animals have lost their homes.

Some day, lots of different animals may disappear forever, like the dinosaurs.

We need to take care of our world and the animals that share it with us, so the story of life on Earth will go on.